DRUMLANRIG

THE CASTLE, ITS PEOPLE AND ITS PAINTINGS

To the memory of
John, 9th Duke of Buccleuch and 11th Duke of Queensberry, KT
1923–2007

INTRODUCED BY THE DUKE OF BUCCLEUCH AND QUEENSBERRY
TEXT BY JOHN MONTAGU DOUGLAS SCOTT
PHOTOGRAPHS BY FRITZ VON DER SCHULENBURG

Foreword

Welcome to Drumlanrig. For at least six hundred years my Douglas forebears have had a foothold in the Nith Valley and for over three centuries this castle has been one of our family homes. For us it stirs the most powerful feelings of contentment. It embraces us in the surround of its hills, evoking a gamut of memories from happy to sad. I hope it is as captivating for you as it is for us, that you will find yourself absorbed in the subtlety of the pale pink stone and its delicate carvings, engaged by the serenity of Rembrandt's *An Old Woman Reading* and intrigued by the thought of the people who contrived to create this magical place.

Drumlanrig is constantly changing. Portraits, like people, move rooms, furniture finds a more sympathetic corner, new acquisitions need to be found a home, fresh eyes see new aesthetic or historical links. This book gives you a snapshot, for the most part through the eyes of a wonderful and thoughtful photographer, Fritz von der Schulenburg, who visited the Castle in 2010. It does not purport to be a guidebook in the traditional sense but instead gives you a glimpse of a great house and those who have lived in it.

Richard, Duke of Buccleuch and Queensberry

SETTING THE SCENE *Midsummer sun lights up the North Front of Drumlanrig, catching its Fontainebleau horseshoe staircase and clock tower. The Castle – an extraordinary stage set of turrets and towers – has hardly been altered since William Douglas, 1st Duke of Queensberry, built it at the end of the 17th century*

Contents

Left The Front Hall
The studded oak front door, with its 17th-century iron yett, or gate, opens into a very civilised front hall full of curiosities. There are visitors' books, an old bagatelle table and Mary, Queen of Scots' needlework. Douglas hearts are stamped on the leather wall coverings

Right The Courtyard in 1950
Until 1834, the Front Hall was a loggia leading onto a courtyard with arches open to the elements. Across the courtyard was a hall (now the Dining Room) with views over the gardens

Drumlanrig and the Dukes of Queensberry

Taking more than a decade to build from 1679, today's castle was superimposed on a 14th-century Douglas stronghold by the 1st Duke of Queensberry. The present Duke looks back on the Castle's history and how his ancestor's vision has continued to shine through the fluctuations of fortune and taste

The many strands of the Douglas family have for centuries been woven through the tapestry of Scottish life, politics and geography. The distinctive family crest – a heart in various guises, but here at Drumlanrig with wings – derives from the loyal promise made to Robert the Bruce by the great Sir James, known as the Black Douglas, that when the king died he would take his heart on a crusade. That forlorn venture ended in disaster in 1330 beneath the Moorish stronghold of Teba in Spain. Surrounded, Douglas sought to inspire his small band of Scots, hurling the casket containing the heart into the midst of the enemy with the battle cry 'Forward, Brave Heart!' The gesture was made in vain. He and his followers almost all perished, but the casket found its way back to its present resting place in Melrose Abbey, and the story has since been a defining part of family history.

Ancient charters tell us that people called Douglas held land around Drumlanrig from 1388 or earlier. Over the subsequent three centuries, as well as Drumlanrig, they created

ABOVE MORTON CASTLE, DUMFRIESSHIRE
The ruined Douglas stronghold of Morton Castle stands on a small loch above Nithsdale. Built in the 13th century, with an enclosed deer park nearby, it continued to be used as a hunting lodge until 1714.
BELOW LEFT *The Douglas emblem, a winged heart*

several strongholds within a 20-mile radius, at Tibbers, at Morton and most particularly at Sanquhar to the north. Their fortunes fluctuated in the era of relative lawlessness and intermittent strife, either with English invaders or other competing clans, that ended only with the unification of the thrones in 1603 in the figure of James VI of Scotland and I of England.

It was in the reign of his grandson Charles II, however, that the family fortunes were put on a firm footing by Sir William Douglas, who forged a career in Scottish politics as one of the Lords of the Treasury and ultimately as Lord High Commissioner. Douglas rose rapidly through the ranks, becoming Earl of Drumlanrig and, in 1684,

the 1st Duke of Queensberry. To accompany his new-found wealth and status, he conceived a magnificent new house, the cross between a castle and a grand mansion that is essentially the Drumlanrig we see today. His son James, who succeeded him in 1695, was an equally significant politician. Known as 'the Union Duke', he played a crucial role in advancing the Act of Union in 1707, which resulted in the consolidation of the Scottish and English parliaments. James and his younger brother Henry had done the Grand Tour, setting off at the ages of 18 and 16, respectively, for two-and-a-half years of travel in France and Italy. Considerable time was spent in Rome, and that influence is seen particularly in the design of the family vault at Durisdeer Church.

Charles, 3rd Duke of Queensberry, was married to one of the more interesting figures in the family's history, Catherine Hyde. Kitty, as she was generally known, was both

SIR GODFREY KNELLER (1646–1723)
William Douglas,
1st Duke of Queensberry (1637–95)
Sir William Douglas rose rapidly to power after the Restoration, succeeding the Duke of Lauderdale, who died in 1682, as the most powerful man in Charles II's Scotland. In 1679 he embarked on building the Drumlanrig Castle we see today. He was created 1st Duke of Queensberry in 1684 and is seen here in the Dining Room in his peer robes, with a coronet on the table to his right

a generous patron of the arts and a formidable free-thinker. Most notably, she took up the cause of John Gay, the poet and author of *The Beggar's Opera*, which was dedicated to her. This radical satirical work caused a sensation when it was first performed in London in 1728. Gay's next production, *Polly*, was banned as a result. Kitty's reaction, which included outspoken criticism of King George II to his face, led to her being barred from the court. She and her husband subsequently spent considerable time at Drumlanrig, and the elaborate garden designs of the 1730s and 40s are perhaps one of the consequences. She continued to court controversy, whether through the unfashionable simplicity of her style of dress or the employment and promotion of a young Negro slave, about whom there was much whispering.

Neither of the two sons of Charles and Kitty survived their parents, and as a result the inheritance passed to a cousin, William, Earl of March, who became 4th Duke of Queensberry. Known to history as 'Old Q', he was a colourful character renowned as

THE SOURCE OF DRUMLANRIG'S SANDSTONE
Drumlanrig's distinctive crystalline sandstone, pale pink and sparkling in dry weather, much darker in wet, comes from a nearby quarry on the other side of the River Nith

a gambler and lecher. He milked his great inheritance, incurring the wrath in verse of both Burns and Wordsworth for cutting down his magnificent woodlands. Drumlanrig itself was left in a sorry state, its roof leaking badly. When he died in 1810, it was without any recognised legitimate heir, although in his own view he had at least a daughter, Maria Fagniana, to whom he gave the considerable fortune on which the great Wallace Collection of art and furniture in London would be founded.

Thus the titles moved sideways again, but this time the Dukedom of Queensberry was to pass through a female line, thanks to the marriage of the 2nd Duke's daughter Lady Jane Douglas to Francis, 2nd Duke of Buccleuch, in 1720. Their grandson Henry, 3rd Duke of Buccleuch, inherited both the ducal title and the bulk of the Queensberry estates. On the other hand, the title of Marquess of Queensberry required a male descent, and it passed instead to a Sir James Douglas, coincidentally a brother-in-law of the Duke's. With it went a much smaller estate near Annan, on which was built a fresh family seat, Kinmont. From that point on, the Marquesses of Queensberry have had their own separate and interesting history, which encompasses the creation of the famous rules

of boxing and the notorious friendship of Lord Alfred Douglas with Oscar Wilde.

Henry, 3rd Duke of Buccleuch and 5th Duke of Queensberry, enjoyed his dual dukedom for only two years, and it was left to his son Charles, 4th and 6th Duke, and his grandson, Walter Francis, 5th and 7th Duke, to undertake the restoration of Drumlanrig and its transformation internally with the addition of furniture and paintings from the enormous Buccleuch collection. This work embraced the transformation of the gardens in the Victorian manner, with acres of greenhouses providing bedding plants and exotic fruits and vegetables on an astonishing scale, only relatively modest traces of which remain.

The scale of activity is all the more remarkable given that the principal homes of the family were to remain Dalkeith, just outside Edinburgh, and Montagu House in London. This remained the case until the 1920s, and it was perhaps only in the last 80 years that Drumlanrig was to take a more central place in the family lives of Walter, 8th and 10th Duke, and his son John, father of the present Duke. Their deep knowledge and love of the working rural estates, farms and woodlands that surround the Castle are perhaps the key to that attachment. During their stewardship, and particularly in the last 30 years, a huge programme of restoration and conservation work has ensured that this historic building is well set for the centuries ahead.

Scottish architectural history has been much enlivened by fresh thinking in recent years about the appropriateness of the term 'castle'. The tendency to link any building that is castellated with endemic warfare and limited civilisation is now being seen as reflecting a Victorian slant on Scottish history that stemmed largely from the novels and poems

DRUMLANRIG CASTLE IN 1953
The North Front, by Felix Kelly, in the Castle's glittering post-war period

of Sir Walter Scott. Instead, there is growing awareness of the extent to which Scotland and its nobility were exposed to the ideas of the Renaissance and classicism, and were less subject – except perhaps in the Border lands – to the threat of repeated violence, and we now know that major buildings were more akin to mansion houses or French châteaux.

Drumlanrig fits this pattern. Though there were earlier castles, including one mentioned in 1429, we have no idea of their appearance. However, the inventories at the death of James, 7th Lord of Drumlanrig, in 1578, do talk of him having 'beildet the haill house and pallice of Drumlanrig', and this must be the building for the enlargement of which we find plans being drawn up in a document of 1618 in the Castle Charter Room. Little, if anything, seems to

have been done at the time, and we have to move forward 60 years to the time of William, shortly to be the 1st Duke, before building works are put in hand. Sadly, no plans or accounts survive, and we can only speculate about who influenced the architecture. Although Sir William Bruce, 'Scotland's answer to Inigo Jones', is mentioned, it seems more likely that those responsible were the King's Master Mason, Robert Mylne, and his son-in-law James Smith, who was to become the leading architect in Scotland at the end of the 17th and beginning of the 18th centuries. Just as important was the builder, one William Lukup, Master of Works at Drumlanrig, who can be seen in a castle doorway on the tomb of four of his children in the churchyard at Durisdeer.

While some traces of the earlier building can be seen in the east wall, the principal block of the house reflects a unified vision and construction that was certainly under way by

1679 and nearing completion in 1689. These are the dates inscribed above windows in the inner courtyard. Three of the sides are of simple, rough-hewn rubble, but the northern front is a breathtaking stage set of dressed stone, classical pilasters, carvings of swags and scrolls and spooky faces, topped with a central clock tower with a massive coat of arms and great ducal coronet. The date on the clock face, 1686, coincides with documents detailing a visit by two Dutchmen, Peter Paul Boyse and Cornelis van Nerven, stone carvers working around this time at Kinross, another great Scottish house. The stage set is reinforced by the horseshoe staircase, which led originally not into the entrance hall but into an open loggia and the huge internal courtyard. The main door to the house was directly opposite, in the south-facing block.

Drumlanrig has remained remarkably unchanged since that great rush of building. In the 19th century, when Old Q's dilapidations were being put right, the loggia was glazed to create a new front hall, and sadly the north-facing Gallery, which ran the entire length of the floor above it, was divided into bedrooms. New service ranges, linking to the forward pavilions on either side of the main entrance front, were added in the orange-tinted stone of Dumfries.

This is not unattractive in itself, but it compares unfavourably with the magical qualities of the local Drumlanrig stone, which is crystalline in character, so that its subtle pale pinkness takes on the mantle at times of a grey, dreich, damp day and at others of a mellow golden midsummer evening. For many people the stone seems to define Drumlanrig, enabling it to float almost mystically in its mountain setting.

The Dukes of Queensberry

Since William Douglas, the 1st Duke, conceived the grand plan for his palace in Dumfriesshire, 11 Dukes have been responsible for its upkeep. And there has been only one bad penny among them

WILLIAM, 1ST DUKE OF QUEENSBERRY (1637–95) *By Sir Godfrey Kneller*

CHARLES, 3RD DUKE OF QUEENSBERRY (1698–1778) *By George Knapton*

WILLIAM, 4TH DUKE OF QUEENSBERRY (1725–1810) *The notorious Old Q, painted as a young man by Allan Ramsay in 1742*

The 1st Duke, Scotland's Lord High Commissioner, is said to have been appalled at the soaring costs of building Drumlanrig. But he had time to enjoy his palace: ousted from office by James II's Catholic party, he retired here for the last nine years of his life. The 2nd Duke, known as 'the Union Duke' for his part in the Act of Union, added the great oak staircase. The 3rd Duke built a vast garden but lost both his heirs. His gambling cousin the Earl of March, 'Old Q', became the 4th Duke. Then, in 1810, he left the house barely watertight to his Scott cousin Henry, 3rd Duke of Buccleuch, who became 5th Duke of Queensberry. His descendants restored the house, and love it and live in it to this day.

JAMES, 2ND DUKE OF QUEENSBERRY (1662–1711) *The famous 'Union Duke' – 'a complete courtier' – by Sir John Medina*

HENRY, 3RD DUKE OF BUCCLEUCH AND 5TH DUKE OF QUEENSBERRY (1746–1812) *Painted in the uniform of the South Fencibles by Quadal in 1780. Henry inherited Drumlanrig in 1810*

JOHN, THE 7TH AND 9TH DUKE
(1864–1935) *By Sir George Reid RA in 1909*

WALTER, 8TH AND 10TH DUKE, AND FAMILY *By Edward Seago, 1938. Duchess Mary side-saddle; Elizabeth (later Duchess of Northumberland) on Threepenny (right); Johnnie dismounted; Caroline (Lady Caroline Gilmour) on Bridget*

LORD ESKDAILL, THE FUTURE 9TH AND
11TH DUKE (1923–2007), AGED SIX
By Charles Edmond Brock, dated 1929

JOHN, 9TH AND 11TH DUKE, WITH HIS FATHER, WALTER, 8TH AND
10TH DUKE (1894–1973) *The late Duke joined the Navy in 1942. His father commanded a battalion of the King's Own Scottish Borderers*

RICHARD, 10TH AND 12TH DUKE (BORN
1954) *The present Duke, painted in 1981, when Earl of Dalkeith, by John Ward RA*

The Drawing Room

Originally the Great Dining Room, Drumlanrig's Drawing Room fills the centre of the south front on the first floor

Drumlanrig's formal rooms are laid out in *enfilade* along the first floor of the South Front, staterooms befitting a ducal palace that are reached by a freestanding oak staircase. The grandest, the Great Dining Room, is now the Drawing Room, gracious but far from stiff. The card tables with jigsaw and backgammon boards still in place show that this room was where the family retired after dinner. It is easy to miss the ornately carved pediments over the doors, vestiges of a grand processional way leading to the

THE PORTRAITS
ABOVE *To the left of the fireplace are James VI and I, with his Queen, Anne of Denmark, by the studio of Paul van Somer; Francis, 2nd Duke of Buccleuch, in blue coat and red breeches, by Allan Ramsay; Out of sight is John, 2nd Duke of Montagu, in scarlet uniform, by John Shackleton.*
OPPOSITE *To the right of the fireplace are the Duke of Monmouth in Garter robes, after Sir Peter Lely; John, 2nd Duke of Argyll, in armour, and Sarah Jennings, Duchess of Marlborough, both by Sir Godfrey Kneller. The portrait of Lady Anne Scott, far right, is attributed to Charles d'Agar*

A CORNER OF THE DRAWING ROOM
Omphale and Hercules support a cabinet of curiosities from Versailles. Its door opens to reveal a painted garden. It may have originally been a gift from Louis XIV to Charles II, who in turn gave it to Monmouth. The monogram of Monmouth's wife, Anne, Duchess of Buccleuch, graces the two fine velvet settees

Withdrawing Room, now Ante-Room, and the State Bedchamber beyond.

Inventories indicate that the room was hung with tapestries. Since 1930, when paintings at Dalkeith Palace and Montagu House were dispersed to Drumlanrig, Bowhill and Boughton, it has boasted full-length portraits of figures in rich attire, including James VI of Scotland and I of England in ruff and breeches, with his pearly Danish bride (page 52); and the Duke of Monmouth

in full Garter regalia. But stealing the show are Charles II's famous gifts to his son Monmouth, the cabinets at either end of the room. Charles's portrait (page 53) hangs above one cabinet, supported by Omphale and Hercules, perhaps by Pierre Golle, of which there is a similar example in the J Paul Getty Museum. The other cabinet, by André-Charles Boulle, is held up by figures of Summer and Autumn, and above it is a portrait of Monmouth.

A CORNER OF THE ANTE-ROOM
The 18th-century velvet covers of a set
of Queen Anne high-back walnut
chairs glow in reflected sunlight in the
Ante-Room. Above them hangs a group
of portraits. The lady painted in the style
of Sir Peter Lely is unnamed. Next to her is
the 1st Duke of Queensberry, attributed to
John Riley. The gentleman in armour at the
bottom left is thought to be the 2nd Duke's
brother; the man on his right, the brother
of Mary Boyle, the 2nd Duke's wife

The Rembrandt in the Ante-Room

Drumlanrig's celebrated Dutch masterpiece

Rembrandt's contemplative late portrait *An Old Woman Reading* hangs against dark oak panelling above the fireplace in the Ante-Room, alongside a 17th-century Brussels tapestry. Dated 1655, the painting was purchased some time before 1770, together with a self-portrait now in the National Gallery in Washington, by George Brudenell, Duke of Montagu. He paid £140. His daughter Elizabeth (page 41), who married Henry, 3rd Duke of Buccleuch, would inherit it along with Boughton House, which has remained in the family ever since. In the centre of the room is a Louis XIV Boulle table inlaid with tortoiseshell and brass. An early 18th-century longcase clock includes phases of the moon and is signed 'John Topping Memory Master'.

REMBRANDT VAN RIJN (1606–69)
An Old Woman Reading, 1655
Perhaps one of Rembrandt's most sublime studies of old age. The light is reflected off the pages of a book and the perspective is such that the painting is designed to be viewed from below, either angled on an easel or high on a wall as here. The room provides the ideal 17th-century setting

PREVIOUS PAGES HOLDING COURT
*Early-18th-century velvet-covered
walnut chairs and a day bed are ranged
along a wall of the Ante-Room*

Bonnie Prince Charlie's bedroom

*With its 17th-century tapestries
and furniture, the State Bedchamber
is still very much of its time*

The State Bedchamber, the last room in the *enfilade* of 17th-century rooms on the first floor, takes its name from an uninvited guest, Prince Charles Edward Stuart, the Young Pretender. His portrait by Liotard with his brother Henry is one of the masterpieces in the Buccleuch collection of miniatures. Bonnie Prince Charlie stayed on December 22, 1745, during his retreat north – to the horror of James Ferguson of Craigdorroch, the 3rd Duke's chamberlain.

The Prince's 2,000 Highlanders bedded down on straw in the Castle, consumed sheep from the park, which they slaughtered at the foot of

*The oak-panelled State Bedchamber
with its 17th-century rosewood bed*

the stairs, bayoneted Kneller's equestrian portrait of William of Orange on the Oak Staircase (page 65) and broke down doors. 'May God grant there may never be any such guests here,' Ferguson wrote to the Duke. Some would say Drumlanrig got off lightly. Brussels tapestries of river landscapes, a Japanese black lacquer cabinet and a colonial rosewood bed with canopy and spiral columns all give the room a strong late-17th-century feel. The high-back chairs are in the manner of Daniel Marot, the Huguenot arbiter of taste at William and Mary's court.

JEAN-ETIENNE LIOTARD (1702–89)
Prince Henry Benedict Stuart (1725–1807) **and Prince Charles Edward Stuart** (1722–88), 1736
Liotard's miniature of the 14-year-old Bonnie Prince Charlie (in red) and his brother is painted in enamel on copper and measures just under 3 inches across. The gentleman in the corner of the bedroom (right) is their father, Prince James Edward Stuart, the Old Pretender

The Great Oak Staircase

Once the free-standing staircase had been added in 1697, the Staircase Hall would become one of the most beautiful rooms in the Castle, filled with Renaissance and post-Restoration paintings

A ccess to the suite of formal rooms on the first floor is by the Great Oak Staircase. The dark panelling and inviting views into the dining room and morning room on the ground floor, and upstairs all the way through the drawing room to Bonnie Prince Charlie's bedroom, make this hall one of the most atmospheric rooms in the castle. Light pours in from the south through three storeys of windows. One disguised door gives as if by magic onto a balcony with steps down to the garden.

When James, the well-travelled 2nd Duke, ordered this freestanding staircase – still a novelty in Scotland – it appears to have extended into what is now the Dining Room, without a dividing wall. The 'barley-sugar' column is of the kind that he would have seen in Rome.

The lower walls of the hall lend themselves perfectly to a group of gem-like Renaissance paintings, including an impressive portrait from the workshop of Hans Holbein the Younger of the ill-fated Sir Nicholas

THE STAIRCASE HALL
LEFT *Looking through to the Morning Room. The area under the stairs is the perfect place to hang small Tudor portraits.*
RIGHT *Initially the lower flight of steps ended in the Castle's original front hall, now the Dining Room*

Carew. Once Henry VIII's Master of the Horse, Carew – here resplendent in shining armour with a cloth-of-gold turban – was executed in 1539.

The upper walls, with their swirling, gilded candelabra, provide an august setting for the royals with whom the 2nd Duke and his Duchess were closely associated. By the door hang a pair of portraits of William of Orange and Mary II (partially obscured by the chandelier). Another portrait of William, the equestrian painting that so irked the Highlanders during the '45 Rebellion, hangs at the foot of the stairs (page 65). William's infidelity and obsession with war games sorely provoked the Queen, whose close friend Purcell is thought to have composed one of the masterworks of English music, *Dido's Lament*, in sympathy. Queen Mary's sister, Queen Anne, seen here enthroned on the far right, presented the Duke with these royal portraits. It is a mark of the esteem in which the Duke and Duchess were held that their portraits by Kneller are on the same scale.

The gallery running round the walls below these portraits appears to be there for viewing purposes only, but in fact one of the portraits conceals a secret passage to the Southeast Tower stairs.

The Staircase Gallery
Mary Boyle, Duchess of Queensberry (to the right of the chandelier) is flanked by the royals William and Mary (on her left) and an enthroned Queen Anne (on her right). The chandelier, with 16 arms in the form of mermaids in the mouths of sea serpents, is 54 kilograms of solid silver. It was made circa 1680, and Robert Garrard added the ducal coronet in 1835. The Boulle bracket clock over the door is one of a pair. At the end of the vista is the State Bedchamber

Renaissance portraits

The upper gallery of the Oak Staircase is hung with the grandees of the Restoration. Downstairs is the courtly art of the Northern Renaissance

OPPOSITE ASSOCIATE OF
HANS HOLBEIN THE YOUNGER
Sir Nicholas Carew (d. 1539)
In addition to armour, Sir Nicholas wears brown slashed breeches and a black cap trimmed with white plume over a shimmering cloth-of-gold turban

BERNAERT VAN ORLEY (C. 1488–1541)
Eleanor of Austria (1498–1558)
Seen here bedecked in jewels, the favourite sister of the Hapsburg Emperor Charles V was betrothed to the future Henry VIII. But when Henry became king, he married her aunt Catherine of Aragon instead. She went on to marry Manuel I of Portugal, who died of the plague, then, in 1530, Francis I of France

CIRCLE OF JOOS VAN CLEVE (C. 1485–1540)
Francis I, King of France
(reigned 1515–47), c. 1530
Francis, arch-rival of Henry VIII and Charles V, and ally of the Ottoman sultan Süleyman the Magnificent, is in his thirties here. Francis convinced Leonardo to move to France, taking the Mona Lisa with him. Francis's father-in-law, Louis XII, owned the Buccleuch Madonna of the Yarnwinder

RIGHT MASTER OF THE MAGDALEN
LEGEND (ACTIVE C. 1483–C. 1527)
Jacques de Vendôme, Prince de Chabanais, Vidame de Chartres (d. 1507)
Vendôme was Louis XII's 'grand-maître des eaux-et-forêts', one of France's most prestigious offices. Here, he is seen in a cap with the badge of the Virgin Mary
FAR RIGHT
JAN GOSSAERT, CALLED MABUSE
(C. 1478–1532)
The Virgin and Child
Mabuse acquired a Leonardo-esque polish when he accompanied Philip of Burgundy to Italy in 1508. He established the custom for Flemish artists to study in Italy, which lasted into the age of Rubens and Van Dyck

The Dining Room

*The sweep of family portraits in the panelled Dining Room
includes four of the first five Dukes of Queensberry*

S tepping through the studded
oak door from the courtyard
into what was once a grand
staircase hall must have created
a tremendous sense of arrival. Filled
with light, the south-facing room has
gorgeous views of gardens vanishing
into the woods. At night, the family
portraits on the panelled walls are lit by
silver William and Mary sconces. At one
end of the room, next to William,
4th Duke of Queensberry (Old Q, who
almost squandered it all), sits the most
powerful man in Restoration Scotland:
the 1st Duke of Queensberry, builder of
Drumlanrig. At the other end of the
room is the 2nd Duke's daughter Lady
Jane Douglas (page 39), who married
Francis, 2nd Duke of Buccleuch – rather
to his grandmother's annoyance – thereby
uniting the Douglases and the Scotts.

ABOVE DUCAL LINEAGE
*William Douglas, 1st Duke of Queensberry,
with the profligate 4th Duke on his left,
surveys the Dining Room from above
the silver wine urn on the serving table.
The good 3rd Duke is to his right (in
the corner), next to Henry, 3rd Duke of
Buccleuch and 5th of Queensberry, the first
Scott to inherit both dukedoms*

OPPOSITE POWERFUL WOMEN
*Women often held the key to Drumlanrig's
story – literally in the case of Lucy Walter,
seen (on the fireplace wall) holding up a
portrait of James, her son by Charles II:
he would marry the Scott heiress, Anne,
and so become Duke of Monmouth and
Buccleuch. Lady Jane Douglas, dressed in
red (over the serving table), would marry
their grandson, the 2nd Duke of Buccleuch.
Her mother, Mary, is next to the fireplace*

The Serving Room

A smell of silver polish pervades the light-filled Serving Room, next to the Dining Room. It now houses portraits of the all-important men who ran the family's palace at Dalkeith

T he huge oak table in the Serving Room is perfect for leaving trays ready to be carried off to the Dining Room next door. The door next to John Ainslie's portrait of the chef Joseph Florence leads to the Southwest Tower and the kitchen and pantry downstairs. Florence cooked for three successive dukes and was much admired by Sir Walter Scott. He is seen pointing to a menu in the portrait – one of a group showing members of the household at Dalkeith Palace in the early 1800s. The painting of a lobster above the handsome range of ovens is by Jan Flyt, the celebrated 17th-century Flemish Baroque still-life painter.

ABOVE *A lobster and a basket of fruit, circa 1643, by Jan Flyt (1611–61)*

RIGHT *The portrait by the door is of the chef Joseph Florence pointing to a menu which lists 'potage a la reine', 'boudins a la Koln', 'gradin a la Drumlanrig', 'croquette a la Montagu', turbot, 'coq de bois rôti' and 'jambon de sanglier'. The silver on the large George III table includes a vase-shaped wine cooler, engraved by Paul Storr in 1812, and a George IV oval dish cover by Robert Garrard, one of a pair made in 1828*

Gentlemen in the Serving Room

Household characters from Dalkeith Palace

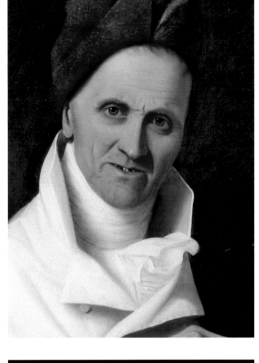

OPPOSITE **The Courier**
The courier to Henry, 3rd Duke of Buccleuch, in red riding coat, white stock and black hat. The name of the handsome courier is not recorded, nor is the artist's, but the style recalls that of Martin Ferdinand Quadal, painter of the Fencible portraits in the Inner Hall

THIS PAGE *Four portraits by John Ainslie, a little-known painter active in Edinburgh between 1815 and 1835. Only 14 of his works are recorded*

TOP LEFT **Baillie William Tait of Pirm**
In black coat and neat white stock, William Tait was the Duke's chamberlain at Dalkeith for more than 30 years from 1803

TOP RIGHT **Joseph Florence**
This famous portrait of the cook to three Dukes of Buccleuch – Henry, Charles and Walter Francis – was painted in 1817

BOTTOM LEFT **Signor Giustinelli**
The dancing master was reportedly aged 113 in 1820, when Ainslie painted him

BOTTOM RIGHT **Major Walter Scott**
This dapper gentleman may have been the 3rd Duke's brother, who died in 1825

The staircase in the Northeast Tower

A tower staircase stands in each of the four corners of the courtyard

A contemporary admirer of the 1st Duke of Queensberry's grand style, described as 'Gusto Grande', wrote that the Palace at Drumlanrig 'is a square Building of fine free Stone, with a spacious Court in the middle, and a Turret, and great Stone Stairs in each Corner'.

The oak staircase completed by the 2nd Duke in 1697 (page 24) was essentially decorative. The tower stairs, on the other hand, were, and remain, the real arteries, providing access to every part of the house without cluttering up any rooms or views. The pale stone steps fanning out from a central stone newel have an almost geometric modernity. The only ornament on the white walls is an elegant black 'iron cord' banister.

Never mind that this was all rather old-fashioned in the 1690s. Drumlanrig was 'an ancient paternal seat'. Like French châteaux, castles in Scotland were still expected to evoke the aura of *noblesse d'épée* (nobility of the sword).

The Northeast Tower
Built between 1679 and 1689, this was the first of the four tower staircases to be started and the last to be completed. The door on the right opens into the courtyard

Portraits of the Duchesses

Remarkable and beautiful women have shaped Drumlanrig's story, from the Restoration to the new Elizabethan age. Their presence brings life to every room in the Castle

Patrick Lichfield captured four generations in his classic 1980s conversation piece. Jane, Duchess of Buccleuch, the present Duke's mother, looks up at her daughter, Charlotte Anne. Elizabeth, Countess of Dalkeith (centre), the present Duchess, looks down at her daughter Louisa Jane, whose great-grandmother, Mary, Dowager Duchess of Buccleuch, wife of the 8th and 10th Duke, smiles out at society's favourite photographer.

Catherine Hyde (opposite) was mistress of Drumlanrig seven generations earlier. She married Charles, the kindly 3rd Duke of Queensberry, and is celebrated by the poet Matthew Prior as *Kitty, beautiful and young / And wild as a colt untamed.* She spent much of her time in the South. Dumfriesshire women annoyed her, as did the Scottish Sabbath, and she was famous for her frankness. She helped to transform the garden, ordering a two-mile-long aqueduct to feed a magnificent cascade. As Prior's poem concluded:
Fondness prevailed, mamma gave way;
Kitty, at heart's desire,
Obtained the chariot for a day,
And set the world on fire.

RIGHT *By Patrick Lichfield (from right): Mary, Dowager Duchess of Buccleuch; Lady Charlotte Anne Scott (Comtesse de Castellane); Elizabeth, Countess of Dalkeith, the present Duke's wife; Jane, Duchess of Buccleuch; Louisa Jane.* OPPOSITE *Catherine Hyde by Jean-Baptiste van Loo, c.1730. This portrait of Kitty, the charismatic wife of the 3rd Duke of Queensberry, hangs in the White Bedroom*

D rumlanrig has been enriched by the convergence of three powerful families – the Douglases, the Scotts and the Montagus – though more by accident than by design.

Francis Scott, 2nd Duke of Buccleuch, was a man not easily swayed. When he brought together the Douglases and the Scotts by marrying the 2nd Duke of Queensberry's daughter Lady Jane Douglas (left, in red) in 1720, it was in defiance of his grandmother. Anne, Duchess of Buccleuch (Monmouth's wife and the builder of Dalkeith Palace), had expected him to marry the daughter of the then more promising Duke of Douglas, confusingly also called Lady Jane Douglas.

It was another 90 years before the two dukedoms and fortunes were united, when their grandson Henry, 3rd Duke of Buccleuch, inherited the Queensberry dukedom as a result of the earlier tragic death of Kitty's children.

By then, Henry's wife, the swan-like Elizabeth Montagu (far right), had already added the Montagu fortune to the pot. Her brother, Lord Monthermer, son and heir of George Brudenell, Duke of Montagu, died in 1770 at the age of 35, three years after her marriage, leaving her heiress to the Montagus of Boughton, but not to the dukedom, which could only pass through the male line and so became extinct.

Adam Smith, the young Duke of Buccleuch's tutor, wrote to the philosopher David Hume telling him of Elizabeth's arrival at Dalkeith as a bride, 'I am sorry you are not here because I am sure you'll fall perfectly in love with her.'

ABOVE *Lady Elizabeth Montagu (1743–1827), after Sir Joshua Reynolds, c. 1755. The wife of Henry, 3rd Duke of Buccleuch, was much admired by Adam Smith. She became the Montagu heiress on her brother's death in 1770, and Duchess of Queensberry when her husband inherited Drumlanrig in 1810*

FAR LEFT *Lady Jane (1701–29) and Lady Anne Douglas (d. 1741), by Sir Godfrey Kneller. This portrait of the daughters of the 2nd Duke of Queensberry – and Kitty's sisters-in-law – is in the Dining Room. Lady Jane (in red) married Francis, 2nd Duke of Buccleuch*

LEFT *Alice Powell, Duchess of Buccleuch (d. 1765), by Thomas Hudson (1701–79). After poor Jane Douglas died aged 29, Duke Francis again followed his own heart by marrying Alice Powell – a slightly scandalous act, as she was not a noblewoman. Seen here dressed in satin and lace, Alice is the subject of one of Hudson's finest portraits*

Philip de László's stunning painting shows the present Duke's grandmother in 1932. Mary Lascelles, or Molly as she was known, a granddaughter of the Duke of St Albans, married Walter, the future 8th Duke of Buccleuch and 10th of Queensberry, and quickly learned to ride side-saddle with great elegance. An earlier portrait of her as a classic Twenties beauty, by Glyn Philpot, is at Bowhill, another of the family residences.

In 1958, the portrait of Jane McNeill, Countess of Dalkeith, wife of the future 9th Duke of Buccleuch and the present Duke's mother, caused a sensation at the Royal Academy: all 14 judges gave it a coveted A, and the painter, John Merton, leapt to fame, although its unfashionable hyper-realism caused a furore in certain circles.

Merton depicts her holding a book with the Scott crest in a classical archway. Above her head is a winged Douglas heart. Beyond are the River Tweed and the Eildon Hills, her new home. In one oeil-de-boeuf above the columns of the classical portico, she holds a white fan-tailed dove from Eildon Hall; in the other, her Siamese cat.

LEFT PHILIP DE LÁSZLÓ
(1869–1937)
Mary, Countess of Dalkeith, 1932
Mary Lascelles was the wife of the future 8th Duke of Buccleuch, who inherited in 1935. The Hungarian-born artist Philip de László succeeded John Singer Sargent as London's favourite portrait painter

ABOVE JOHN MERTON (B. 1913)
Jane, Countess of Dalkeith, 1957
John Merton said it took 1,500 hours to
paint this celebrated portrait of the
26-year-old Jane McNeill, Countess
of Dalkeith, wife of the future 9th Duke of
Buccleuch. It provoked heated debate in
the art world when it was unveiled in 1958

The Morning Room

Drumlanrig's charm lies in the informal small rooms, especially the Morning Room, with its deep sofas and morning sun

Drumlanrig may be imposing outside, but inside it is surprisingly intimate. Two of the loveliest, most feminine rooms are the Morning Room, in the southeast corner of the house, and the adjoining Parlour. It is round these two rooms that life in a more relaxed age revolves. Piles of inviting books and a roaring fire tempt you to spend the day curled up in a deep sofa or armchair. Window recesses offer the chance to complete a jigsaw, play cards or simply admire the splendid views.

After the dark oak panelling of the staircase hall, the refreshing aquamarine walls make a wonderful backdrop for eight luminous, understated Paul Sandby watercolours of Windsor Great Park, an elaborate giltwood Queen Anne mirror over the writing table, and the porcelain figurines on the William and Mary gilded corner brackets. The colour also sets off to perfection the pearly pink taffeta worn by Jane, Countess of Dalkeith, seen over the fireplace, and the white satin and coral bow of Queen Henrietta Maria's dress on the wall opposite (overleaf). The ceiling's plasterwork, with its Douglas hearts, dates from the 1840s.

THE MORNING ROOM
John Merton's portrait of the Countess of Dalkeith hangs above the fire. Chintz curtains frame the deep window recesses

LEFT *The Morning Room faces east and south and is filled with the morning sun. Over the writing table is a Queen Anne giltwood mirror. The topographical studies by Paul Sandby are of the Great Park at Windsor*

BELOW *The room served as a small dining room for the Duke's agent in the early 19th century, when the pilastered recess framed a sideboard. The 18th-century prints either side of Henrietta Maria are of 17th-century court costumes and are embroidered with actual fabrics. They used to hang in a room known as 'the Court of France' – a letter of 1846 describes the Duke walking about in it 'singing French chansons out of tune'*

OPPOSITE CIRCLE OF SIR ANTHONY VAN DYCK
Queen Henrietta Maria (1609–69)
Seen here in a delicate silk dress, Henrietta Maria was Charles I's beautiful French Queen. This is a version of the portrait in the Royal Collection painted by Van Dyck

The Parlour

House parties in the Fifties and Sixties always had tea in the Parlour. The room now has a group of the Castle's loveliest portraits

The Parlour is similar in atmosphere to the Morning Room next to it: and indeed a secret door connects the two. The paintings on the warm coral walls include two 17th-century portraits by Sir Peter Lely, which hang above the baby grand piano. These have been chosen for the sumptuousness of the garments rather than for the sitters' identities. One shows Jane Myddleton, a society beauty who was known to Pepys, in the role of the goddess Ceres; the other shows an unknown woman (quite possibly Mrs Myddleton again) posing as the goddess Diana. By the door is a theatrical portrait of Sophia Campbell, Baroness de Clifford, by Sir Joshua Reynolds.

There is also a self-portrait of Sir David Wilkie, painted in 1811, which shows the great Scottish painter as a shy and intense young man from Fife. The other self-portrait, an enigmatic likeness, is of the 17th-century artist John Riley.

TOP RIGHT *The baby grand piano.*
RIGHT *Self-portraits of John Riley (1641–91) and Sir David Wilkie (1785–1843).*
LEFT *'Diana' by Sir Peter Lely*

The Boudoir

A world apart from the rest of the house, the Boudoir forms an apartment on the first floor with the White Bedroom

During the Second World War, when a girls' school moved into part of Drumlanrig, the Boudoir became the family sitting room, full of gossip, newspapers, books and dogs. After the war, the Morning Room directly below became the centre of daily life. The walls are similar in colour to the Morning Room's, but the elegant damask-and-giltwood Louis XV canapés give it a French 18th-century feel.

The stars of the room are the cabinet paintings, the most important being Dutch and Flemish, including a Ruisdael wooded landscape and a Wouwerman stag-hunt. There is also a portrait after Daniel Mytens of Charles I and Henrietta Maria departing for the chase, with the dwarf Jeffrey Hudson, and their horses and spaniels (page 60).

A short, curving panelled passage through the thick wall opens into the gallery of the Oak Staircase (page 26). A second door provides access to the Southeast Tower and a third, 'secret' door leads to the White Bedroom.

ABOVE IN THE FRENCH MANNER
Giltwood Louis XV canapés by Jean Lebas stand either side of a tiled fireplace. An 18th-century portrait of Anne Boleyn hangs between the deeply recessed corner windows. The room is also called 'the Duchess's Boudoir'

OPPOSITE THE CABINET PAINTINGS
Above the table are important landscapes and genre paintings, including a moonlit river by van der Neer, a drinking scene by van Ostade and card players by Teniers. A capriccio by Louis XVI's sister, Madame Elisabeth de France, is over the commode.
RIGHT *'Kermesse', a luminous carnival scene by Jan Brueghel the Younger (1601–78)*

The White Bedroom

Four duchesses and a room with a view

This bedroom, with its many shades of white, has glorious views over the River Nith. It last belonged to Mary, Duchess of Buccleuch, grandmother of the present Duke. Molly, as she was better known, loved to walk her black spaniel in the hills of Drumlanrig. Her portrait by de László, painted in 1932 (page 42), hangs on one side of the bed. On the other is Kitty Queensberry (page 38), the firebrand who antagonised George II. A portrait of an older, wiser Kitty, arms folded, hangs next to the fireplace. Two further Duchesses share this coolly elegant room, with its rope-trellis wallpaper by Cole & Son and pale-grey

damask sofas. Over the marquetry bureau is Gainsborough's masterful 1768 portrait of Mary, Duchess of Montagu. A remarkable connoisseur, she was the wife of the 3rd Duke of Montagu, who bought the Rembrandt. On her right is the previous Duchess of Montagu, Lady Mary Churchill, daughter of the great Duke of Marlborough.

DUCHESSES IN THE BEDROOM
Over the bed: the great beauty Mary ('Molly'), Countess of Dalkeith (1900–93), wife of the future 8th and 10th Duke, by Philip de László, and fearless Kitty, Duchess of Queensberry (1701–77), by van Loo. Above the bureau, from left: an unnamed daughter of John, Duke of Argyll, perhaps Lady Dalkeith, by an

artist in the circle of William Hoare of Bath; the distinguished Mary, Duchess of Montagu (1712–75), by Thomas Gainsborough; a pastel by Francis Cotes of Lady Mary Churchill, Duchess of Montagu (1689–1751), in a vivid blue dress. Her profile, attributed to Kneller, is next to the fireplace; on the other side is a pastel of Kitty Queensberry by Catherine Read

The independent Duchess

Patronage of John Gay, author of 'The Beggar's Opera', led to a family rift with George II

Lady Catherine Hyde is the best documented of all the early Duchesses. She and her husband, Charles, 3rd Duke of Queensberry (portrayed on the cover of this book), are remembered for completing the magnificent gardens at Drumlanrig begun by the 1st Duke. In van Loo's oil painting of 1730, the Duchess is still the impetuous young 'Kitty' of Prior's poem. She tragically lost both their sons in her early fifties, the first in a shooting accident, the second from consumption. In Catherine Read's portrait (left), she is a stoical but still beautiful older woman.

Kitty and her husband were staunch patrons of the poet and dramatist John Gay, who is recorded at Drumlanrig in 1729 picking the best books from the library to take back to London. In the dashing portrait of the 3rd Duke in red coat and leopard-skin waistcoat, Gay's portrait leans against a pedestal. His satirical ballad opera *The Beggar's Opera* caused a sensation, running for a record 62 nights at Lincoln's Inn Fields. The prime minister, Sir Robert Walpole, who is caricatured in it, had its sequel, *Polly*, banned. Outraged, Kitty asked George II to intervene. The King refused and barred Kitty from court. She told him she would be happy to stay away.

LEFT *A rare oil portrait by Catherine Read (1723–78) of Kitty Queensberry after the death of her two sons. Scottish-born, Read established herself as a society portraitist in London, painting Queen Charlotte and the Prince of Wales among others.*
RIGHT *English jugs, bowls and foot basin with a washstand of the kind that Kitty would have had at home in Burlington Gardens in London or at Drumlanrig*

Room 39

Under the clock tower, what was once an enormous gallery was divided into a long passage with bedrooms in the 1830s. One, known simply as Room 39, has its own extraordinary sitting room

The North Gallery ran from tower to tower, with windows north, south, east and west, quite a promenade for a wet day. On Sir Walter Scott's advice, it was chopped up into bedrooms, which still have their original moiré wallpaper. Under the clock tower is a sliver of a sitting room with an exuberant fireplace from Dalkeith Palace. Jane, Duchess of Buccleuch, restored it to its Victorian splendour. On the desk under John, 7th Duke of Buccleuch, is a photograph of his daughter Princess Alice, Duchess of Gloucester, who married George V's brother, Prince Henry. A lively writer, in *Memoirs of Princess Alice, Duchess of Gloucester* she describes a visit to her grandfather, the 6th Duke, in 1909:

'My grandfather loved to have children around and Sybil and I were the lucky ones chosen to be with him during his stay at Drumlanrig… After tea the grown-ups would rush about with us in games of hide 'n seek or pounce piggy, a Scott variation in which two people hid and ambushed the rest. They seemed to enjoy it as much as we did. The four towers of staircases and three floors of long passages gave plenty of exercise and we must have run miles during the course of an evening.'

A VERY VICTORIAN SITTING ROOM
The marble fireplace and overmantel were installed at Dalkeith in the early 1700s by Anne, Duchess of Buccleuch. At Drumlanrig they frame a portrait of Catherine of Braganza. The flower painting is by Jean-Baptiste Monnoyer, the portrait of John Charles, 7th Duke of Buccleuch, by Sir George Reid. Opposite it, though not visible, is a plaster profile of Walter Francis, the great Victorian 5th Duke of Buccleuch

The Royals in the story

The story of Drumlanrig is entwined with the history of Restoration Scotland, and the castle is full of royal portraits

Mary, Queen of Scots denounced 'Drumlanrig young and old' as the 'hellhounds, bloody tyrants, without souls or fear of God' who helped depose her in 1568. If it is true, as tradition suggests, that she and her ladies-in-waiting embroidered this panel, it is ironic that it graces the Front Hall of Drumlanrig Castle.

By 1617, when her son King James and his Queen visited Drumlanrig, relations between the Stuarts and the Douglases had healed.

In the Civil War, the Douglases were firmly Royalist, and the 1st Duke of Queensberry's father was imprisoned and ruinously fined by Parliament. The 1st Duke revived the family fortunes after the Restoration.

Needlework panel of the late
16th or early 17th century
*This romantic depiction of a queen with
her attendants, soldiers and cavorting
lions in a hilly landscape is said to be by
Mary, Queen of Scots and her ladies-in-
waiting, and the date of the needlework
fits the story. It hangs over the fireplace
in the Front Hall, in an 1830 frame
decorated with the Royal Scottish arms*

The 2nd Duke consolidated them by backing William and Mary even before the Bloodless Revolution of 1688, then by supervising the Act of Union in 1707, for Queen Anne, which forestalled a Jacobite Restoration in Scotland after her death. By 1745, when Bonnie Prince Charlie marched in, the Stuarts were simply an embarrassment.

The visit to Drumlanrig in 1617 of King James and his Queen does not explain the presence of their portraits in the Drawing Room. The early Stuart portraits originally belonged to Anne, Duchess of Buccleuch, and were hung prominently at her palace at Dalkeith, outside Edinburgh. In Anne's eyes, Stuarts were family, even if Monmouth – Charles II's son and her unwise husband – ends up on a platter as John the Baptist's head in one painting. To this day, the Scotts of Buccleuch have the right to wear the Royal Stuart tartan.

LEFT AFTER DANIEL MYTENS
King Charles I and Queen Henrietta Maria departing for the chase
In this delightful portrait in the Boudoir (a small-scale version of a work in the Royal Collection), horses are led up to the King and Queen, who are surrounded by dogs. A water spaniel waits on the right. The Queen's dwarf, Jeffrey Hudson (far left), was known as 'Lord Minimus'

LEFT STUDIO OF PAUL VAN SOMER
**King James VI of Scotland
and I of England** (1566–1625)
*In this portrait in the Drawing Room,
James, in embroidered pink coat, breeches
and lace ruff, holds the Badge of the
Garter. On the table are his crown, orb
and sceptre. James is best remembered
for the Authorised Version of the Bible –
still considered the finest flowering of the
English language. Van Somer (1577–1622)
was his favourite court painter. Van Dyck
would follow in his footsteps*

FAR LEFT STUDIO OF PAUL VAN SOMER
**Anne of Denmark, Queen of
Scotland and England** (1574–1619)
*James's Queen wears an embroidered silk
dress with matching shoes and sparkling
pearls and holds a plumed fan. Although
her husband considered her frivolous for
her love of masques, Anne was a patron of
the arts, supporting both the playwright
Ben Jonson and the architect Inigo Jones*

RIGHT SIR PETER LELY AND STUDIO
King Charles II (1630–85)
*A portrait of Charles II, in armour with
a lace cravat, hangs above one of the two
cabinets he gave to his son, the Duke of
Monmouth and Buccleuch. A twin portrait
of Monmouth hangs above the other cabinet*

**James, 2nd Duke of Queensberry
and 1st Duke of Dover** (1662–1711)
*By Kneller. 'The Union Duke' oversaw the Act
of Union, which united Scotland and England*

William III (1653–1708)
Above and opposite *By Kneller. With
Queen Mary, the Protestant William
of Orange deposed Catholic James II in
the Bloodless Revolution of 1688*

Queen Anne (1665–1714)
*A grateful Queen Anne gave this portrait by
Kneller to the 2nd Duke, along with paintings
of her husband and of William and Mary*

Queen Mary II (1662–94)
*By Kneller. William of Orange's wife and
Queen Anne's sister, Mary became the
Stuarts' Protestant alternative to James II;
the 2nd Duke was an early supporter*

Mary of Modena (1658–1718)
*The Queen Consort of Charles II's brother
and successor, James II, by Willem Wissing.
Their Catholicism cost them the throne*

The Duke of Monmouth and Buccleuch
(1649–1685)
*Charles II's son, painted by Lely, boldly
attempted to seize his uncle James II's
throne. His haste cost him his head*

The Inner Hall and Armoury

This small hall is hung with family portraits and Fencible and Militia memorabilia

When you enter the castle, it is a relief to find lots of pleasingly small rooms. The well-lit passages were an innovation, replacing the traditional draughty open floor plan.

The Inner Hall, which leads off the Front Hall, is in the Northeast Tower, where early plans show a chapel. In the centre of the photograph above is Derek Hill's 1970 portrait of Walter, 9th Duke of Buccleuch and 11th Duke of Queensberry, wearing the uniform of Captain-General of the Royal Company of Archers, the Queen's Bodyguard in Scotland. The painting hangs above his ceremonial sword and arrows in an alcove leading to the Duke's study. The walls of the hall are hung with memorabilia of the Militia and Fencible regiments formed by the 3rd Duke.

ABOVE *Scottish basket-hilted broadswords and an early-18th-century targe, or shield, covered with hide and brass studs, can be seen on the right. The four muskets with socket bayonets are late-18th-century fusils*

HENRI-PIERRE DANLOUX (1753–1809)
Sergeant Mather in the uniform of the Dumfries Militia
Signed and dated 1799 by the French émigré artist Danloux, who worked for the 3rd Duke of Buccleuch at Dalkeith. The label under this painting reads: 'The perfect specimen of a British grenadier'

The Fencible and Militia regiments

Henry, 3rd Duke of Buccleuch, raised the Southern Regiment of Fencible Men in North Britain at Dalkeith in 1778. It came to be known as the South Fencibles and consisted of a grenadier, a light infantry and eight battalion companies, 1,120 men in all, drawn from Edinburgh, Dumfries and the Borders. They volunteered for service in any part of Britain and in 1779 were guarding French prisoners of war in Edinburgh Castle. The regiment was disbanded in 1783.

In a portrait by Quadal, the 3rd Duke appears in front of his regiment on a grey charger at a military review outside Edinburgh (see page 10). Quadal, a Moravian émigré, also painted the Duke's eldest son, Charles, Earl of Dalkeith – wearing the same red uniform, with its distinctive gosling-green facings – in the park at Dalkeith, then still the principal family seat.

The Duke also helped to raise the Dumfries Militia (later the 10th North British Militia and 3rd Battalion of the Royal Scots). Two portraits of militia sergeants in action by Danloux hang in the Inner Hall, outside the Duke's study.

MARTIN FERDINAND QUADAL (1736–1808)
Charles, Earl of Dalkeith, in Fencible uniform, with his brother Henry, 1779
Quadal's charming portrait of the sons of Henry, 3rd Duke of Buccleuch, in the park at Dalkeith includes their pet monkey, Jacko (in fact an ape), and their mother's dogs Toby

and Jim. Charles would become 4th Duke of Buccleuch and 6th of Queensberry, playing a key part in rescuing Drumlanrig after Old Q's neglect. Qadal and Danloux were two of the emigrés who arrived in Dalkeith at the time. Refugees from the French Revolution would swell their ranks. The 3rd Duke was known for his hospitality

THE SOUTH FENCIBLES
ABOVE *Two South Fencible soldiers painted by an artist in the circle of David Morier.*
FAR RIGHT *Two portraits attributed to Alexander Nasmyth (1715–1840): a South Fencible officer (top) and the 3rd Duke in South Fencible uniform with the Star of the Order of the Thistle*

LEFT HENRI-PIERRE DANLOUX
Sergeant Stevenson in the uniform of the Dumfries Militia
This picture of a sergeant firing a musket was one a pair of militia sergeant portraits painted for their commander, Henry, 3rd Duke of Buccleuch

The Charter Room and West Passage

Unchanged in appearance, the Charter Room still has its iron door and oak-lined walls

The Charter Room appears in the earliest plans of the present house, midway between the State Bedchamber in the Southwest Tower and the North Gallery (now the North Passage). It was here that the 1st Duke kept the all-important charters proving his ownership of the Castle and his estates. The iron inner door was intended to keep out not people so much as fire. Groin vaults support a stone ceiling, as in the bedroom directly beneath it – described in 1694 as 'My Lord Duke's Study'. In the Charter room there is a foliaged boss where the ribs meet, in the 'Study' a Queensberry crest. Early Drumlanrig inventories and plans are still kept in the Charter Room.

To S.W. Tower. Drawing Room, & To North Passage.

LEFT *A massive key unlocks the original 17th-century iron door of the Charter Room. The door is designed to preserve the room's contents from fire*

RIGHT *Inside the Charter Room, still used to store records, the groin-vaulted ceiling is in its original unplastered state. The room below, the Duke's study is also vaulted in stone*

ABOVE *The West Passage, with windows onto the courtyard, led from the staterooms to the Gallery (now the North Passage). Oak wainscoting, white walls and the painting of a man-of-war saluting the fleet, by a follower of Peter Monamy (1681–1749), give it the air of a Dutch interior. Above the doorway is a 17th-century Douglas heart carved in wood*

FAR LEFT *The door to the Northwest Tower. Useful directions for confused guests*

The Southwest Tower and Basement

Pure architecture is reduced here to bare, beautifully proportioned essentials

Many a house guest with a less-than-perfect sense of direction has been found wandering up and down the wrong stairs at Drumlanrig. Understandably, for all four towers appear identical, except that in the case of the Southwest Tower, the walls are unplastered and display smoothly pointed stonework. Given the quality of the masonry, it is easy to see how the 1st Duke's bills for Drumlanrig must have mounted up. The stepped ceiling gives the stairs an even more sculptural feel. Dates above windows outside each of the four towers show how the building progressed between 1679 and 1689. The Southwest Tower was completed in 1685.

These handsome oak armchairs, with their high spindle backs and rush seats, are mid-Victorian. They stand in a stone-flagged, whitewashed basement passage outside the Old Servants' Hall in the east service wing, which Charles, 4th Duke of Buccleuch, added in the early 19th century.

LEFT *The Southwest Tower staircase, its pink sandstone still visible.*

OPPOSITE *A pair of elegant Victorian chairs in a stone-flagged basement passage*

The heart of the Castle

Off the long Basement passage, some of it 16th-century,
are the rooms essential to a well-run household

Drumlanrig's ingenuity lies in its pragmatic floor plan: a simple square, hollow in the middle, encircled by rooms. The Basement has an uninterrupted passage all the way round, which gives it easy access to all four towers and the passages leading off them. Since the castle occupies a mound, the courtyard is higher than the surrounding Basement, and skylights are needed for the passage. All manner of useful rooms open off it – the Kitchen, Scullery, Pantry, Flower Room, Linen Room, Brushing Room and a large Drying Room full of hot pipes, indispensable in Dumfriesshire. Most of these rooms have large windows and views over the parkland and woods.

LEFT THE BASEMENT PASSAGE
Betty Cook rounds a corner in the
Basement passage, lit from behind by
a glazed door to the garden, where herbs
grow in a suntrap under the south wall.
Generations of Scotts have been brought
up on her legendary cooking. The indent
in the passage marks the lower walls
of the earlier 16th-century fortification

RIGHT THE OLD KITCHEN
Bedroom candlesticks stand on a Regency
pine table in the Old Kitchen, with
its latched door and sturdy cupboards.
An Arts and Crafts oak ladderback
armchair stands in the corner

ABOVE AND FAR RIGHT
THE FAMILY ARCHIVES
Each generation faces a new
challenge and the archives are once
more a priority. Here Professor
David Munro, former director of
the Royal Scottish Geographical
Society, peruses maps in the
old wine cellar, where light and
humidity can be carefully controlled

RIGHT CURTAIN RAILS
Laid out on the threadbare carpet of
an old bedroom, ready to be reused

ABOVE CHINTZ GALORE
*Spoilt for choice, the interior decorator
Alison Graham sifts through two
centuries of surplus chintz on the billiard
table. The patterns offer an invaluable
resource for contemporary designers*

LEFT AND FAR LEFT OLD FRIENDS
*Handsome armchairs and a Victorian
day bed await the upholsterer.
Old trunks reveal secrets. One of these
contained the riding clothes worn
by Mary, Duchess of Buccleuch, in
Edward Seago's family portrait (page 11)*

Stepping out into the landscape

The Sundial Terrace on the South Front is like a box in a grand natural amphitheatre

When you step onto this terrace from the Dining Room, the view comes as a great surprise. Stairs lead down to what is thought to have once been a series of Renaissance hanging gardens. One garden was called 'Barbados', another 'Virginia', inspired by plant-hunting expeditions to the Americas.

By the 1740s, many of the terrace walls had been pulled down to create one huge Baroque garden, with gentle slopes and unbroken vistas (page 86). Facing the South Front was a cascade which fell into a canal. By 1810, thanks to Old Q, all this was in ruins.

In the 19th century, Walter Francis, 5th Duke of Buccleuch, for 18 years president of the Royal Horticultural Society, replaced it with an extravaganza of parterres. His High White Garden is seen here, but fortunately without the gleaming white sand that gave it its name.

ABOVE *Mary, Duchess of Buccleuch, on the Sundial Terrace in 1950, with her cocker spaniel Fancy*

RIGHT *The bronze sundial, dated 1692, is inscribed with the Queensberry crest and directions to points from Dublin to Mecca. The balustrade of thistles and roses was made by James Horn of Kircaldy in the 1680s. It is the only decoration on the Castle's austere South Front*

LEFT *The balustrade includes a handsome Douglas heart design*

FOLLOWING PAGES *During the Second World War, the East Terrace was ploughed up for potatoes, then grassed over after the war. The present garden, planted in 1978, was laid out with topiary conifers according to the 1738 plan*

Views of Drumlanrig

The view in February 2010 across the Nith Valley (opposite top) is little changed since William Leitch made his watercolours in 1843–44 (above and opposite left), though the woods felled by Old Q have recovered. The Nith (opposite right) was painted by Philip Sheppard c. 1858.

The study of the avenue by an unnamed guest (left) is inscribed 'From my window at Drumlanrig, September 29, 1855'.

The grand plan

A 17th-century palace in a Georgian paradise

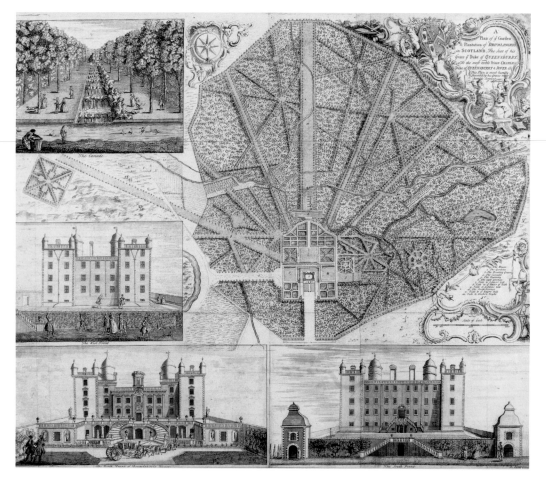

A Plan of ye Garden and Plantation of Drumlanrig by the Huguenot-born landscape surveyor John Rocque is the most important visual record of the castle in the early 18th century. Rocque's 1739 engraving was made for Volume 4 of the *Vitruvius Britannicus*, a great survey begun by the architect Colen Campbell in 1715. Rocque's plan – with south at the top – maps out rides and avenues radiating from all four fronts. The gardens created by the first three Dukes of Queensberry, and later abandoned by Old Q, culminate in the 3rd Duke's cascade on the hill to the south (top left). Served by an aqueduct two miles long, it drops down in steps to a canal in full view of the castle. The North Front (below) is seen without its later wings, its staircase forecourt neatly contained by balustrades. Pavilions with ogee roofs flank the South Front (left).

Rare impressions

Drumlanrig's pink walls and silvery domes should have inspired centuries of watercolours, yet surprisingly few are known. The delightful example above was painted by Alexander Patterson in July 1893, with an architect's mastery of perspective. Some of the profuse greenery has since been removed and the window frames been painted white. Little else has changed. The work on the left, a later copy of an 18th-century watercolour, depicts the East Front of the Castle, with a pavilion identical to those seen in Rocque's *Plan* (opposite).

The watercolours

The park at Drumlanrig still shares the
ordered beauty of Paul Sandby's studies of
Windsor Castle in the Morning Room
(above). Sandby (1725–1809) acquired his
skill as a draughtsman surveying the
Highlands after the '45 Rebellion. *The
Enchanted Tree* (left) is by the illustrator
Dickie Doyle, a cousin of Sir Arthur
Conan Doyle, painted in 1873. In the East
Corridor, a group of sketches of incidental
country scenes by Thomas Rowlandson
(1756–1827) includes *The Scots Greys*
(opposite) and *A Man Driving a Wagon* (top
right). The country scene with a woman
riding a horse (top left) is by Peter Le Cave.

Stone carvings
Ornament 'as wild as it is lavish'

The entrance front, as Mark Girouard noted in *Country Life*, is 'the showpiece of the house'. Above the stairs is 'a display of Renaissance ornament as wild as it is lavish' carved by Peter Paul Boyse and Cornelis van Nerven. Under the clock tower, inscribed 1686, is a 'great sprouting Queensberry coat of arms'. Curtains, seaweed scrolls and swags of fruit tumble over the arches, and spooky faces look down from above the windows.

Up on the roof
The turrets of Drumlanrig

Scottish country houses are distinguished from most of their English counterparts by their dramatic silhouettes. Drumlanrig's, with its 17 elegant ogee turrets, is one of the most romantic. The 1618 plan for rebuilding the original stronghold had been greatly refined by 1679, when building began. The four huge square corner towers were reduced to more classical proportions, without detracting from the beauty of the silhouette.

The elasticity of lead gives the metal great longevity, but even good lead roofs have to be replaced every 150 years or so. In 1812, after Old Q left the castle derelict, the roof was patched up using lead obtained by melting down statues in the garden 'in a large huge iron pot'. When Drumlanrig's roof was relaid in the 1980s, the work took more than a decade to complete.

DRUMLANRIG'S FAIRY-TALE ROOF
The view from the Northeast Tower, looking over the Castle's lead domes and giant chimney stacks to Nithsdale. The family standard flies in the north wind

Durisdeer and the Queensberry Aisle

Drumlanrig Castle stands in the parish of Durisdeer, a tiny village across the Nith Valley with a wonderful secret

Two miles from the Castle, the parish church of Durisdeer stands in a cluster of houses on the old road to Edinburgh. The medieval church was rebuilt by the 3rd Duke in the 1720s. On one fine tombstone in the graveyard is a relief of a man with a chisel in one hand, a mallet in the other: he is William Lukup, the Master of Works who built Drumlanrig. Adjoining the church is the vault known as the Queensberry Aisle, where the first Dukes of Queensberry are buried. Modest in size, it is amazing in concept.

*The work of two Dukes
of Queensberry, the
1st and the 2nd, this
elaborate memorial comes
as a total surprise when
one enters it from the
simple country graveyard.
The magnificent marble
'baldacchino' with
barley-sugar columns
over the crypt is worthy of
Bernini. Ordered by the
1st Duke in 1694, it now
acts as a frame for the
fanciful memorial
depicting James, the
2nd Duke, and his wife,
Mary, erected in 1713.
The sculptor, the great
John van Nost, received
the princely sum of £400
for the work. His model,
carved in wood, is
preserved at Drumlanrig*

Modern landmarks

The Andy Goldsworthy installations

The internationally acclaimed Andy Goldsworthy – sculptor and photographer – lives in the area, and his work can be found across the Nithsdale landscape. This stone cone, the *Penpont Cairn*, was created to mark the new millennium. Most recently, in 2009 he constructed the *Striding Arch* out of the Castle's pink sandstone in the middle of the Marr Burn, hidden from sight in the Drumlanrig woods.